A J&K PRIMER

From Myth to Reality

B. G. Verghese

India Research Press
Centre for Policy Research

India Research Press
B-4/22, Safdarjung Enclave, New Delhi - 110 029.
Ph.: 24694610; Fax : 24618637
contact@indiaresearchpress.com ; bahrisons@vsnl.com
www.indiaresearchpress.com

2007

ISBN -10 : 81-8386-039-7
ISBN -13 : 978-81-8386-039-0

Under the auspices of the Centre for Policy Research, New Delhi.

Cataloguing Publication Data

A J&K PRIMER
From Myth to Reality
B.G. VERGHESE
The views presented in this volume are solely those of the author and not of the CPR.

Includes references and bibliography.
1. Jammu / Kashmir 2. South Asia 3. Himalaya 4. J & K 5. LOC 6. Pakistan
7. Autonomy 8. Siachen 9. PAK / Northern Areas 10. Indus 11. Terror/Jihad
I. Title II. Author

Printed for *India Research Press* at Focus Impressions, New Delhi -110 003

CONTENTS

A J&K PRIMER

Introduction

Jammu and Kashmir is a contentious and emotional issue that has been with us since Independence. It has two aspects. The first is internal, concerning relations between the people of J&K and the Indian State. The other is external and entails Pakistan's aggressive role in the matter that India took to the UN Security Council on January 1, 1948. The people of J&K are obviously an interested party but not a third party.

After years of trial and tribulation, a peace process is under way with the people of J&K as well as with Pakistan. At this juncture it is necessary to be clear about the background, sequence of events, issues in contention and related matters. With the passage of time, there is danger of basic facts being ignored or forgotten. Myth has tended to obscure reality.

Any enduring settlement must rest on facts, not sentiment and emotion, though these cannot be altogether ignored. Pakistan and some sections of the international community have their own perceptions about the Kashmir Question. For influential elements in the West, this was driven by cold war considerations and Pakistan's role as a "frontline state" from the early 1950s, which in some ways remains a continuing reality. Inconvenient facts were expendable. However, perceptions matter and it is therefore important that misperceptions and imagined truths do not cloud debate and projected solutions, howsoever reasonable.

India stands on firm ground, though mired in some of its own follies. It has been singularly inept in presenting its case from the very start, only to have the discourse and attendant vocabulary hijacked by others to its own discomfiture.

Yet it is in India's highest interest to end this sorry chapter and bring the J&K question to a just and honourable resolution that accommodates legitimate points of view. It must therefore be generous and prepared to make concessions. However, it will find it difficult to convince its interlocutors at home and abroad about the merits and reasonableness of its stance unless the cobwebs are swept away.

Some will say that rehearsing the past will lead to recrimination and thereby vitiate the climate of goodwill and trust that alone can move the peace process forward. On the other hand, talks will go nowhere unless there is clarity about what precisely one is discussing and there is a common point of departure.

This J&K Primer is intended to educate ordinary people

Note: The Indian part of the erstwhile Princely State of Jammu and Kashmir State is in this text referred to as J&K and the Pakistan controlled areas as Pakistan Administered J&K (PAK) and the Northern Areas (NA). The terms "Azad" or Pakistan Occupied Kashmir (POK) have been avoided.

everywhere about the basics of the Jammu and Kashmir question and to put various events and issues in context. It does not purport to be an elaborate political history of J&K or a scholarly critique of the issue. Nor does it seek to indulge in barren polemics. Rather, it aims to present a series of snapshots that tell the central story of J&K post-1947. Pakistani and UN references have been cited in preference to Indian or other sources in order more convincingly to sweep away the humbug that underlies much contention.

The degree of ignorance about J&K in both India and Pakistan, and around the world, is quite astonishing. Literature about the beginnings of the conflict in 1947 is not easily available in India today and much discourse and even policy making appears to rest on mere say-so and self-serving narratives. There is as much to unlearn as to learn. India's motto is Satyameve Jayate. This Primer is immodestly designed to lend Truth a helping hand.

Land and People

The erstwhile Princely State of Jammu and Kashmir has since 1949 been a divided territory, with India in control of Jammu, Kashmir and Ladakh. The Muzaffarabad area (PAK) and the Northern Areas are under de facto Pakistan administration. In addition, China controls the trans-Karakoram Shaksgam Valley and adjacent region, which Pakistan unilaterally ceded to it in 1963 as part of a boundary settlement, and also Aksaichin and a strip of Western Ladakh, into which it intruded and then militarily occupied in 1962.

Kashmir, as much as Jammu, has been part of India's political and cultural domain and spiritual consciousness for some 3000 or more years going back to the Mahabharata legend. The Ganpatyar and Khir Bhavani Temples in the Valley, the Shankaracharya shrine dominating Srinagar and the giant Buddha statues in Gilgit speak of this connection. The Emperor Asoka brought Buddhism to Kashmir in the 3rd century B.C and it was here that Kanishka held the Third Buddhist Council. Lalitaditya's reign (697-738 A.D) marked a golden age. Islam was adopted by consent in the 14th century giving birth to a vibrant, syncretic sufi-rishi tradition of Kashmiriyat that has been deliberately undermined by today's jihadis.

J&K is a highly plural multi-ethnic and multi-lingual entity. The ethnic stock on the Indian side is principally made up of Dogras, Punjabis, Kashmiris, Gujars and Bakarwals, Ladakhis and Baltis while those living on the other side are of Punjabi, Pathan, Balti, Dardi, Shin, Yashkun, Mongol, Tadjik, Turkic and other Central Asian extraction.

The LOC represents a fairly well defined ethno-cultural divide, notwithstanding some Punjabi, Balti and other overlap. No ethnic Kashmiris live in PAK.

The Princes

Under the Partition settlement and Indian Independence Act, enacted by the British Parliament, the Princely States would become notionally independent with the lapse of paramountcy on August 14/15, 1947. However, given historical, cultural, economic and strategic compulsions and the obvious logic of contiguity, the Rulers were advised by the last Viceroy, Mountbatten, that they had little option but to join either of the two new Dominions of India or Pakistan. This would entail signing an Instrument of Accession ceding control over External Affairs, Defence and Communications to the Dominion of choice. Further entrustment of powers was left to negotiation.

The Congress urged that in case of any doubt regarding accession, the wishes of the people must be taken into account in whatever manner feasible. The Muslim League was adamant that the choice of the Ruler be deemed final.

On the eve of Independence, practically all the 565 odd Princely States had acceded to one Dominion or the other, after some politicking in certain cases. Only a few continued to waver. The contrasts are noteworthy.

(a) **Hyderabad,** with its 80 percent Hindu majority, was completely embedded within British Indian provinces that were indisputably poised to become part of the new Dominion of India. (See map of Undivided India). The State had absolutely no option other than to join India. The Nizam's efforts to seek Dominion Status (Independence) against self-evident popular opinion, with strong Pakistani backing, was misconceived and mischievous and was inevitably short lived. The Nizam appointed Mir Laik Ali, a former Pakistan representative to the United Nations, as President of his Executive Council. Soon thereafter, he advanced a loan of Rs 20 crores to Pakistan in the form of Government of India securities and appointed a Public Relations Officer in Karachi! Towards the end of August 1948, he invoked the good offices of the United Nations and a Hyderabad delegation travelled to New York via Karachi. However, the growing communal depredations and belligerence of the Nizam's armed Razakars compelled India to launch a Police Action against the State on September 15. The Hyderabad forces surrendered two days later and the Nizam cabled the Security Council on September 25, 1948 withdrawing his case before the UN. Pakistan's hand was clearly discernible in this entire chain of sorry events. (See V.P. Menon, "Integration of the Indian States". (Orient Longmans, 1956).

(b) In Baluchistan, the Khan of **Kalat**, the head of an association of Sirdars outside British Baluchistan, opted for independence on August 15, 1947, a decision endorsed by the Baluch legislature on January 4, 1948. However, the Khan was compelled to submit militarily and Kalat was annexed by Pakistan in April 1948. Both

Kalat and **Bahawalpur** had toyed with accession to India but were rebuffed by Delhi on obvious grounds of geography and the composition and wishes of the population. (See Penderel Moon, P. 107 "Divide and Quit". Chatto & Windus, London, 1961).

(c) The position of **Junagadh** was peculiar. Situated on the Kathiawar coast 300 miles from Pakistan, it had an overwhelming Hindu population and was part of a crazy quilt of princely territories with fragments embedded within one another. Thus bits of Junagadh were enclaves within other states such as Baroda, Gondal and Nawanagar. (See map). Grafted on this political jigsaw was a shared infrastructure. Nevertheless, the Nawab of Junagadh reneged from a common understanding that this clutch of Kathiawar princes would accede to India and threw in his lot with Pakistan. A new Dewan, Sir Shah Nawaz Bhutto, appointed in May 1947, was in correspondence with Jinnah who advised him to hold out until August 15. This he did and then announced accession to Pakistan on that day (H.V.Hodson "The Great Divide". Hutchinson. London, 1969). The accession was not accepted by Pakistan until September 13, plunging the state into confusion. Pakistan refused a referendum. The Nawab fled to Karachi towards the end of October in the wake of mounting popular protest and administrative collapse and Sir Shah Nawaz Bhutto finally invited India to take over. This was done on November 9,1947. A referendum on February 20, 1948 gave Pakistan 130 votes against over 220,000 for India! (See V.P. Menon, "Integration of the Indian States". (Orient Longmans, 1956).

(d) Maharaja Hari Singh of **Jammu and Kashmir** could not make up his mind whether to accede to Pakistan or India. Therefore, on the eve of Independence, he entered into a Standstill Agreement with Pakistan for the maintenance of essential supplies like food, salt, kerosene and petrol and railway, telegraph, banking and other services. Notwithstanding this agreement, Pakistan attempted to strangulate the State economically in the face of the Maharaja's detailed protests and finally invaded it on October 20-24, 1947 with the assistance of armed tribal marauders from the NWFP.

J&K was nominally independent between August 15 and October 26, 1947 when it acceded to India.

(e) Maharaja Ranbir Singh gained suzerainty over **Chitral** by treaty in 1874 and the Mehtar (Ruler) paid annual tribute to J&K until 1947. (P.N.K. Bamzai, "A History of Kashmir" Metropolitan Book Co, Delhi, 1962). Thereafter the principality was absorbed by Pakistan, which subsequently incorporated it in NWFP. India never challenged this fait accompli.

Pakistan's Invasion and J&K's Accession

With the raiders advancing on Srinagar, the Maharaja appealed for Indian assistance to repel the aggression.

India agreed but sought a legal basis through accession after consultation with the Sheikh Abdullah, the popular Kashmiri leader. The Maharaja signed the Instrument of Accession on October 26 and, following its formal acceptance, Indian troops were airlifted to the Valley the next morning. The battle was joined.

Despite its pleading innocence and helplessness in turn, the world, including the United Nations, found Pakistan guilty of aggression. Apart from eyewitness accounts of the invasion in the international press, direct evidence is available from several official Pakistan sources. Akbar Khan, then Director Weapons and Equipment, GHQ, Pakistan, (later promoted Major General and appointed Chief of General Staff), assisted and subsequently led the Pakistani forces. He later gave a graphic first person account of the military plans and operations, which he confirms had the blessings and support of Pakistan's top leadership. (See his "Raiders in Kashmir," republished in India by Army Publishers, Delhi, 1990).

In the beginning of September 1947, he writes, "Mian Iftikharuddin (of the ruling Muslim League) arrived in Murree ... and asked me to prepare a plan... to get Kashmir's accession to Pakistan." Akbar Khan prepared such a plan and was soon thereafter called to Lahore "for a conference with the Prime Minister of Pakistan, Mr Liaquat Ali Khan ... attended among others by the Finance Minister (Mr Ghulam Mohammad), Mian Iftikharuddin, Zaman Kiani,

Khurshid Anwar, Sardar Shaukat Hayat (a Punjab Minister)" . Two sets of plans to attack J&K were discussed.

"After the Prime Minister's conference, I returned to Pindi. The first shots had been fired and the movement soon began to gather weight....I cannot say exactly when it was decided that an attack by tribesmen should be carried out in the manner that it was. I had, however, been hearing that Khurshid Anwar was gathering a lashkar of tribesmen... According to (Allen Campbell Johnson's) "Mission With Mountbatten", the Commander-in- Chief, India, received a telegram on 20 October from GHQ Pakistan Army (then commanded by Gen Frank Messervy), stating that some 5000 tribesmen had attacked and captured Muzaffarabad and Domel". From there they advanced on Srinagar via Uri and Baramulla.

The story of Britain's connivance with Pakistan's adventure in J&K is narrated in Chandrashekhar Dasgupta's "War and Diplomacy in Kashmir" (Sage, 2001). He cites copiously from recently declassified British archival material relating to that period. Narendra Singh Sarila's " The Untold Story of Partition" (Harper Collins, 2005) carries this narrative forward with further details of Britain's pre-and post-Partition conceptualisation of Pakistan as a frontline state).

The UN's own verdict in 1950, speaking through Sir Owen Dixon, its Representative in J&K, is unambiguous:

"When the frontier of the State of J&K was crossed, on I believe on 20 October 1947, by hostile elements, it was contrary to international law, and ... when, as I believe, units of the regular Pakistan forces moved into the territory of the State, that too was inconsistent with international law".

UN Resolutions

India went to the UN on January 1, 1948 with a complaint of aggression against J&K by Pakistan under a non-binding Article 35 of Chapter VI of the Charter pertaining to the pacific settlement of disputes through mediation. Within weeks, Pakistan filed a counter-complaint and had the title amended from "The Jammu & Kashmir Question" to "The India-Pakistan Question", attempting to obfuscate what it now calls the core issue. Junagadh was specifically mentioned in the Pakistani plaint and Hyderabad figured in its arguments.

A Security Council resolution of January 17, 1948, called on both sides to "improve the situation" in J&K and to " inform the Council immediately of any material change in the situation". Three days later, the Council further resolved to set up a UN Commission for India and Pakistan and directed it to "proceed to the spot as quickly as possible", investigate the facts and exercise a mediatory influence.

The UNCIP, moving in slow motion, finally arrived in

Karachi on July 7, 1948 when, in the words of one of its members, Josef Korbel of Czechoslovakia, it was met with a "bombshell". (See Korbel, "Danger in Kashmir", Princeton University Press, 1954) This was the bland disclosure that three brigades of the Pakistan Army had been engaged in operations in J&K since the first week of May 1948. The object, it was said, was limited to preventing the Indian Army's spring offensive spilling westward across the border into Pakistan. But soon thereafter, the Pakistan Army swept through Baltistan, knocking at the gates of Leh hundreds of kilometres to the east!

The key UN resolution of August 13, 1948 proposed a Cease Fire Order (Part I), barring any augmentation of armed forces, organised or irregular, followed by a Truce Agreement (Part II) calling for wholesale withdrawal of all Pakistani troops as well as the tribal invaders and other Pakistani combatants from J&K. The territory so evacuated was to be administered by the Local Authorities (of the State) under the surveillance of the UN Commission with such Indian military assistance as might be considered necessary by the Commission. The bulk of the Indian forces would thereafter be withdrawn from the State subject to such numbers as may be required to safeguard peace, law and order. On implementation of Parts I and II, steps would be taken under Part III to ascertain the will of the people regarding the future of the State, as elaborated in a further UN Resolution adopted on January 5, 1949.

The operative part of the January 5, 1949 Resolution reads: "A plebiscite will be held when it shall be found by the Commission that the ceasefire and truce agreement set forth in Parts I and II of the Commission's Resolution of 13 August, 1948 have been carried out and arrangements for the plebiscite have been completed". These arrangements were to include the return of all those who had fled the State following the disturbances.

The Truce terms set out by the Commission on May 2, 1949 specified that they were "without prejudice to the territorial integrity and the sovereignty of the State of Jammu and Kashmir". Consistent with this stipulation, the same communication provided for defence of the Northern Areas by India should this be found necessary by the Government of India and agreed to by the Commission.

Far from withdrawing, Pakistan consolidated its position in those parts of J&K under its control in total disregard of the UN Resolutions. A Pakistan-US military pact was mooted in the autumn of 1953 and a Mutual Defence Assistance Agreement was signed on May 19, 1954. Thus Pakistan violated both Parts I and II of the key August 13, 1948 Resolution with impunity.

The UN Representative, Gunnar Jarring's final report of April 29, 1957 noted that "the implementation of international agreements of an ad hoc character, which has (sic) not been achieved speedily, may become progressively more difficult because the situation with which they were to cope has tended to change". In other words, the UN Resolutions had been rendered effete.

Pakistan's Gilgit Coup

Prior to Independence, the State of J&K was administratively divided into four parts: Jammu, Kashmir, Ladakh, and Gilgit. Gilgit was acquired by Maharaja Gulab Singh in 1846 and was permanently annexed to J&K in 1859.

Given the imperatives of the Great Game, Britain aimed to shut out Russian influence south of the Pamirs and accordingly assumed political and military oversight of the Maharaja's northern territories including Gilgit, Hunza and Chitral. In 1935 the British leased the Gilgit Agency, carved out of Gilgit, from the Maharaja for a period of 60 years, without derogation of J&K's sovereignty over the territory. The Gilgit Agency was formally restored to the Maharaja of J&K with the impending transfer of power in 1947 and the Maharaja's representative, Brigadier Ghansara Singh, took charge in Gilgit a few days before Indian Independence. (See P.N.K.Bamzai, "A History of Kashmir", Metropolitan Book Co, Delhi, 1962).

On October 28, 1947, two days after J&K had acceded to India, the Gilgit Scouts, under the command of Major

William Alexander Brown, a serving British officer seconded to J&K, staged a coup, imprisoned the Maharaja's Governor, Brigadier Ghansara Singh, and declared in favour of Pakistan. The Pakistan flag was hoisted on November 2 and a representative of Pakistan flew to Gilgit on November 14, 1947. A farcical "accession" of Hunza and Nagar, both feudatories under the suzerainty of J&K, followed some weeks later.

Gilgit and the Frontier Illaquas of Hunza, Nagar, Punial, Yasin, Kuh, Ghizar, Ishkoman and Chilas were subsequently amalgamated with that part of Baltistan under Pakistan's occupation to constitute the Northern Areas (NA). Thereafter an Agreement was reached between the Government of Pakistan, the so-called Azad Kashmir (PAJK) Government and the AJK Muslim Conference in Karachi on April 28, 1949, whereby administrative control over NA was entrusted by AJK to the Pakistan Government for the time being in view of its administrative and logistical infirmities. The Muzaffarbad government's prayer before the PAJK and Pakistan Supreme Courts (1991-93) was that the Karachi Agreement lapsed with the enforcement of the (P)AJK Government Act 1970 and that NA must be restored to it. However, the Pakistan Supreme Court ruled that NA was certainly part of J&K but not under the jurisdiction of the PAK administration.

Operation Gibraltar, 1965

Pakistan was frustrated by the failure of the six rounds

of Swaran Singh-Bhutto talks on J&K through 1963 but sensed opportunity in India's discomfiture in the 1962 Sino-Indian conflict. Further, encouraged by its own boundary settlement and friendship treaty with China (1963) and having tested its new US-aided military prowess in Kutch (1964) and also banking on what is saw as a weakened India after the death of Nehru, Pakistan embarked on its next adventure, "Operation Gibraltar". So-called Pakistan "irregulars" with full military support launched a multi-pronged invasion of J&K on August 5, 1965 along five major axes under the directions of Major-General Akhtar Hasan Malik, GOC 12 Division. The objective was to cut off the Indian Army's lines of communication and fan a general uprising in J&K, which would then be followed by a full fledged military assault on Aknoor on August 31, code named Operation Grand Slam.

The Report of General Nimmo, the Australian head of the UN Military Observer Group, to the .UN Secretary General, U Thant, documented Pakistan's transgressions between August 5 and September 2 in specific detail, listing incursions across the LOC. On September 6, Indian forces responded across the Punjab border. A 16-day war ensued, followed by the Tashkent Declaration brokered by the Soviet Union.

Contrary to Pakistan's expectations, not a single person in all of J&K rose to assist the invader. Operation Gibraltar was a fiasco though trumpeted as a great victory.

Recalling this "unnecessary war", on September 6, 2005, the 40th anniversary of Operation Gibraltar, Air Marshal Nur Khan, the then Pakistan Air Chief, spoke to The Dawn of Karachi in these terms: " (The Army) planned Operation Gibraltar for self-glory ... It was a wrong war. And they misled the nation with a big lie that India rather than Pakistan had provoked the war and that we were victims of Indian aggression". He went on to describe the 1971 and Kargil wars as products of the same Army mindset.

Altaf Gauhar, Ayub's alter ego and Information Secretary, writes that India's military humiliation by China in 1962, the death of Nehru, Pakistan's growing friendship with China and its imagined triumph in the Rann of Kutch led Zulfikar Ali Bhutto and Aziz Ahmed (Secretary-General) to dream up a swift short campaign in another bid to seize Kashmir. Ayub Khan ordered the Foreign Office, in collaboration with GHQ, to prepare a plan in complete secrecy to "defreeze" the Kashmir issue. Even the two other service chiefs and corps commanders were kept out of the loop. The adventure was foredoomed to failure. Propaganda bred self-delusion and, Gauhar remarks, "conscience had certainly yielded to wilful fabrication". (See "Ayub Khan, Pakistan's First Military Ruler" by Altaf Gauhar. University Press, 1996).

Cease Fire Line to Line of Control

The Cease Fire Line (CFL) is a product of the Karachi

Agreement of July 27, 1949 signed by the military representatives of India, Pakistan and the United Nations in accordance with the UN Resolution of August 13, 1948. This marked a line running from Manawar in the south, to "Khor, thence north to the glaciers" through the last cited grid reference, NJ 9842, some 23 km north of Khor.

Boundary formation is a three-phase process of delineation (broad definition), delimitation (more specific detailing) and demarcation (marking on the ground). The Karachi Agreement Sections II B clauses (a)-(d) demarcated the CFL all the way up through Khor to NJ 9842. The portion beyond was delineated, "thence north to the glaciers" (a directional terminology frequently used throughout the Agreement), but left to be subsequently demarcated. This was not done as it was probably assumed that the J&K Question would soon be settled and it might not therefore be necessary to undertake the difficult and arduous task of demarcating the Line beyond NJ 9842 which lay in an unpopulated and treacherous glaciated region of the High Karakoram that was yet relatively unexplored and had witnessed no fighting.

The immediately following Section II-C of the Karachi Agreement specifically provides that "The ceasefire line described above shall be drawn on a one-inch map (where available)....so as to eliminate any no man's land". This injunction is critical as it precluded gaps and ambiguities in defining the Cease Fire Line, placing its completeness and integrity beyond question. If such a line is drawn through "Khor, thence north to the glaciers" via NJ 9842, the Siachen snout, from which the Nubra river issues, and by far the larger part of this 75 km long glacier falls on the Indian side of the Line. (See map).

Under the auspices of the United Nations' International Geophysical Year in 1956-58, the Geological Survey of India led a series of major inter-disciplinary scientific expeditions to the Siachen region and took extensive glacier measurements in the Nubra and Shyok Valleys. This was elaborately recorded by the GSI. (B.G. Verghese, "Himalayan Endeavour". The Times of India, Bombay, 1964. See also "From Surprise to Reckoning", The Kargil Review Committee Report. Sage. New Delhi, 1999).

After the 1971 war, it was agreed that both sides keep the territory captured across the CFL. Thus, in the north, India gained 254 sq km in the Turtok sector west of Khor and NJ 9842. These changes in the CFL were duly recorded in the Suchetgarh Agreement of December 1972 under the terms of the Simla Accord. The new Line was accordingly demarcated and certified by the two military commanders in two elaborate sets of maps and re-designated as the Line of Control.

Shaksgam Valley

In 1963, Pakistan unilaterally conceded to China some

5000 sq km of J&K territory in the Shaksgam Valley and adjacent areas of J&K, north of Siachen, from east of K2 to a point a little short of the Karakoram Pass. Thereafter it commenced extending its lines of communication eastwards from Skardu.

The Sino-Pakistan Agreement of March 2, 1963, claimed that "in view of the fact that the boundary between China's Sinkiang and contiguous areas the defence of which is under the actual control of Pakistan has never been formally delimited, the two parties agree to delimit it on the basis of the traditional customary boundary line, including natural features, in a spirit of equality, mutual benefit and friendly cooperation".

Article 6 of that same Agreement states: "The two parties have agreed that after the settlement of the Kashmir dispute between Pakistan and India, the sovereign authority concerned will reopen negotiations with the Government of the Peoples Republic of China on the boundary, as described in Article Two of the present agreement, so as to sign a formal boundary treaty to replace the present agreement...".

Lines of Contention in J&K

There are several "lines" in J&K and it is necessary to distinguish between them.

There is first the international boundary between J&K

and Pakistan in the Jammu-Sialkot sector. This is known as the "Working Border" in Pakistan's terminology and came into being with Partition. Next, the Cease Fire Line, CFL, (Karachi Agreement, July 27,1949), was redesignated as the Line of Control (LOC) in 1972 (Suchetgarh Agreement). The extension of the LOC beyond NJ 9842 in the Siachen sector is, in Indian parlance, known as the Actual Ground Position Line (AGPL). This was established in 1984. The segment east of the AGPL up to the Demchok region in southeast Ladakh controlled by or bordering on China came to be known as the Line of Actual Control (LAC) after 1962. The LAC is currently the subject of boundary negotiations between India and China.

Autonomy and Integration

With J&K's accession to India in 1947, it was necessary to define their constitutional relationship. This was done by adoption of Article 370 of the Indian Constitution, defining the mechanism for managing Centre-State relations with specific reference to J&K. This Article has nothing to do with J&K being part of India or its further "integration with India".

Article 1 and the First Schedule of the Constitution govern integration. Article 1 says that the Union India shall comprise "the States and territories ... as specified in the First Schedule". This Schedule lists J&K, which is defined as "the territory which immediately before the commencement this Constitution are (sic) comprised in the Indian State of Jammu and Kashmir".

More or less "autonomy" therefore does not imply less or more "integration" as mistakenly supposed.

Article 370

Article 370 provides that "(1) Notwithstanding anything in this Constitution ....

(b) i. the power of Parliament to make laws for the State shall be limited to those matters in the Union List and the Concurrent List which, in consultation with the State, are declared by the President to correspond to matters specified in the Instrument of Accession....

ii. Such other matters in the said Lists as, with the concurrence of the Government of the State, the President may by order specify.

(c) The provisions of Article 1 and of this Article shall apply to that state subject to such exceptions and modifications as the President may by order specify; provided that no such order... shall be issued except in consultation with the government of the State

Some critics argue that since Article 370 refers to the J&K Constituent Assembly's consent in matters of consultation, no change could legally be effected after that constituent assembly ceased to exist in 1956. This is a mistaken premise as the constituent assembly was succeeded by a valid State legislature with constituent powers under the J&K constitution.

The Supreme Court in 1984 held in Khazan Chand versus the State of J&K that J&K "holds a special position in the constitutional set up of our country". It went on to explain the ambit and meaning of Article 370 and the Constitution (Application to Jammu & Kashmir) Order 1950, promulgated on January 26, 1950 in accordance with the provisions of Article 370 and opined that it was thus that "the basis for a constitutional relationship between the Union and the State was defined".

Rigged Elections

Elections were held to elect the J&K constituent assembly in 1951. The Muslim Conference commanded support in the Muzaffarbad area and it is perhaps not just by accident but possibly by design that the Indian Army's autumn offensive in 1948 stopped short along what was to become the Cease Fire Line in the Poonch-Rajouri-Akhnoor sector. There was no doubting the immense popularity of Sheikh Abdullah and the National Conference he headed in the Indian administered part of the State, with Ladakh and most of Jammu rooting for India. Yet, sad to say, the elections were rigged.

Some 73 of the 75 seats were won uncontested by the ruling party following the "withdrawal" of all other candidates. The argument that these other candidates voluntarily withdrew for fear of the ire of the electorate or respect for the Sheikh does not hold water. Nonetheless, there was little doubt that even in a fair poll, the National Conference would have won hands down.

Sheikh Abdullah was arrested in August 1953 on charges of secretly seeking independence and hobnobbing with the United States and others to this end. He was disillusioned by the rise of communal forces in Jammu under the Praja Parishad and elsewhere in India under what was to become the Jana Sangh. This gave a new twist to developments in J&K. Bakshi Ghulam Mohammad took over and successive elections in the Valley were rigged in 1957 and even after 1962 when the responsibility for elections in J&K passed from the State election machinery to the Central Election Commission. It is highly unlikely that the loss of some seats in the Valley or elsewhere would ever have reduced those elements favouring India to a minority. This was conclusively proved in what were eminently free and fair elections in 1977 and even in 1983 and quite dramatically earlier in 1965 when no one in any part of J&K rose in support of the Pakistani intruders during the abortive Operation Gibralter.

A blatant return to rigging in 1987, limited though it may have been, marked a turning point in J&K, triggering insurgency some years later in a world resounding to the cry of freedom in the wake of the fall of the Berlin Wall and a succession of freedom movements in Romania, the Philippines, Burma, Nepal and elsewhere and the dramatic collapse of Soviet Communism.

J&K Constitution

J&K alone of all the Indian States has a constitution of its own. This initially provided for a legislative assembly with 100 seats, 25 of these being reserved for the Pakistan-administered areas. The J&K component has since risen to around 87. There is, however, an organic nexus between the Indian and J&K Constitutions.

The preamble to the J&K constitution, drawn up "in pursuance of the accession of this state to India', and more specifically Section 3, specifies that "The State of J&K is and shall be an integral part of the Union of India". The reference is to the entire erstwhile princely state.

Section 5 provides that the executive and legislative power of the State "extends to all matters except with respect to which Parliament has power to make laws for the State under the provisions of the Constitution of India".

The provision for amending the Constitution (Section 147), clearly stipulates that "no bill or amendment seeking to make any change in (a) this Section; or (b) the provisions of Sections 3 and 5; or (c) the provisions of the Constitution of India as applicable in relation to the State shall be introduced or moved in either house of the legislature".

Section 10 of the J&K Constitution vests permanent residents of the State with the fundamental rights guaranteed by the Indian Constitution. The provisional fundamental rights adopted during the drafting stage probably incorporated wider gender rights than that found in the Indian Constitution but did not entrench property rights to the same extent as the latter. This enabled J&K to abolish big landed estates without compensation to effect India's most radical and most successful land reforms.

The J&K Constitution also defines state subjects (permanent residents) who alone may vote and hold property in the State. This has left several thousand so-called Chhamb refugees stateless over two or more generations. The Indian Constitution too has special provisions for the indigenous Bhutia and Lepcha population of Sikkim. Himachal until very recently barred purchase of property by non-state residents while Schedules 5 and 6 prohibit the alienation of tribal lands.

Presidential Orders extending the Indian Constitution to J&K

The 1950 Presidential Order included two schedules

specifying Parliament's competence to legislate for the State. The first schedule specified 35 Union entries under the heads of Defence, External Affairs and Communications plus two modified entries pertaining to the Railways and audit. The State and Concurrent Lists were excluded and all residuary powers were vested with the State. The second schedule extended the Centre's powers to certain other matters including the appellate jurisdiction of the Supreme Court.

Some basic decisions having been taken subsequently by the J&K Constituent Assembly, Central concurrence and further incorporation or exemptions were effected under the Delhi Agreement of July 24, 1952. The State would have its own flag in addition to the national flag. The Sadar-i-Riyasat would be elected by the State legislature but would be a person acceptable to the Centre and be appointed by the President. Dr. Karan Singh thus became J&K's first Sadar-i-Ryasat. The Centre's emergency powers were limited to defence against external aggression under Article 352, but with a proviso that in regard to internal disturbances its promulgation would be "at the request or with the concurrence of the government of the State".

The 1952 Agreement and certain other matters settled by the J&K Constituent Assembly after Sheikh Abdullah's arrest in September 1953 were incorporated in the Indian Constitution through a Presidential Order of May 14, 1954. Indian fundamental rights would apply, subject to such "reasonable restrictions" as the State legislature might deem reasonable.

The customs barrier between J&K and the rest of the country was removed just prior to the promulgation of the 1954 Order.

Further Extension of Union Powers

The J&K Constitution came into force on January 26, 1957. Over the ensuing years Union powers were extended. Financial arrangements included listing J&K as a special category state entitled to 90 (earlier 70) per cent grant and 10 (earlier 30) per cent loan. A State cadre of IAS/IPS officers was created and the jurisdiction of the Auditor and Comptroller-General, Election Commission and Supreme Court fully extended in 1958, 1959 and 1960 respectively.

The permit system that restricted entry of Indian nationals from other parts of the country to J&K was abolished on April 1, 1959. Inner Line Pass regulations, however, still apply in some parts of the Northeast.

Since 1954 around 43 Constitution (Application to J&K) Orders have been issued incorporating several changes, some of a routine character. However, in 1964, the Emergency Articles 356 and 357 were extended to J&K A year later, the State enacted legislation adopting the nomenclature Governor and Chief Minister for Sadar-i-Riyasat and Wazir-e-Azam.

The Governor has since been nominated by the President, as elsewhere, and is not elected by the State Legislature. The appointment and tenure of judges and oaths of office were similarly brought on par with that prevailing in the rest of the country, and the new oath included an affirmation to "Uphold the sovereignty and integrity of India".

In 1985 the Union's residuary powers were restored under Article 248 and Entry 97 of the Union List.

Again in 1985, Articles 339 and 342 were made applicable with modifications enabling appointment by the Union of a commission to report on the welfare of Scheduled Castes and to enumerate those to be listed as Scheduled Tribes in J&K.

In 1986, Article 286 was made applicable, enabling the Rajya Sabha by a two-thirds majority to resolve that Parliament may in the national interest enact legislation under the State List. In 1989, the 10th Schedule pertaining to defections was made applicable to the State.

1975 Agreement

Restored to office in 1975, Sheikh Abdullah discussed with Indira Gandhi developments since his ouster, following upon which G. Parthasarathi and Mirza Afzal Beg were asked to undertake a detailed review. The outcome was recorded in the 1975 Agreement.

The six-point Accord reaffirmed Article 370; vested residuary powers in the State while empowering Parliament to make laws to protect the sovereignty and integrity of India; stipulated that Indian constitutional provisions applied to the State with modifications might be altered or repealed on merits if so requested, provided that laws made by Parliament extended to the State since 1953 under the Concurrent List may be amended or repealed; required the President's assent for any State legislation or constitutional amendment impinging on the appointment, powers and immunities of the Governor, the superintendence, direction and control of elections by the Central Election Commission, eligibility for inclusion in the electoral rolls without discrimination, adult suffrage and the composition of the legislative council. Differences remained on restoring the nomenclature of Sadar-i-Riyasat

A number of Indian laws made applicable to J&K over the years were scrutinised but were found to be largely innocuous. These laws typically related to welfare measures or mundane issues such as registration of books, insurance, child labour, the grading and marketing of agricultural produce, motor vehicles, minimum wages, labour welfare, trafficking in women, etcetera. Indira Gandhi was later amenable to restoration of the usage Wazir-e-Azam through an appropriate amendment to the J&K constitution.

It is noteworthy that adjustments in Centre-J&K

relations have primarily been made through Presidential and Administrative orders rather than by means of constitutional amendments. The same route is therefore available for retractions, if any, that might be agreed upon in the future.

Centre-State Relations

Further leverage was acquired by the Centre through planning and administrative processes and in exercise of its financial and regulatory powers: licensing of industries, import-export and foreign exchange controls, Plan approvals, matching grants, determination of royalties and allocation of small savings. Such erosion of States' rights has evoked protest from all States. The Finance Commissions and the Planning Commission have disposed of some issues. Others were looked into by the Sarkaria Commission on Centre-State Relations.

The J&K Government made certain submissions before the Sarkaria Commission. It favoured greater State control over the all-India services and maintained that the Inter-State Council would be a better vehicle for dealing with Centre-State frictions and misunderstandings. It found the Planning Commission "overbearing" and felt the Centre had stretched the concept of public interest to bring a large sector of industry within the Central sphere.

Economic reform, de-regulation, disinvestment, opening up to private investment and market forces, joint ventures, public-private partnerships and globalisation have brought about marked change. However, pushing autonomy too far could be problematic for a State confronted with harsh terrain and climatic features that add to investment and maintenance costs.

Turning Point: 1984 and 1987 Follies

Sheikh Abdullah was restored to office in 1975 and was returned to power at the head of the National Conference after the 1977 election in J&K. The poll was rated absolutely fair and free by domestic and international observers alike.

The Sheikh passed away in 1982 and was succeeded by Farooq Abdullah who led his party to victory in the 1983 elections but earned the wrath of the powers that be in Delhi by consorting with the opposition National Alliance. Followed his ouster on Delhi's bidding through defections and the induction into office of the short lived Ghulam Mohammad Shah Ministry whose collapse led to the imposition of President's rule. This sorry chapter was followed by fresh elections in 1987 in which the National Conference - Congress alliance once again quite needlessly rigged the elections being contested by a new post-Independence generation, many under the banner of the newly formed Muslim United Front.

These deplorable events marked a turning point. It radicalised the youth, disillusioned by India's seeming lack of commitment to democracy and secularism when it came to J&K. This gave birth to cross-border exfiltration to PAK. Pakistan trained, armed and infiltrated cadres belonging to the JKLF and, thereafter, the Hizbul Mujahideen and other "tanzeems" back across the LOC along with other "guest" militants to launch insurgency in J&K. This was the beginning of the proxy war and cross border terror, with Talibans and jihadis following in their wake post-Afghanistan. (See Appendix)

Over 150,000 Pandits left the State in what is one of the worst cases of ethnic cleansing anywhere. An estimated 50,000 or more Kashmiri Muslims and their children also fled the State, mostly from the Valley, to avoid threats, harassment, extortion, abductions, forced marriages and militant press-gangs. They wished to pursue their businesses and enable their children to study in peace. In so doing they discovered a new India and a new world beyond the Bannihal.

Security Situation

Militancy/insurgency gradually changed from being primarily indigenous, though trained and assisted by Pakistan in the early 1990s, to being dominated by foreign or "guest" militants and jihadis by 1994. Many smaller indigenous militant formations have dissolved, merged or surrendered and the JKLF proclaimed it had abandoned arms. The major indigenous militant group still active is the Hizbul Mujahideen. President

Musharraf banned six terrorist organisations in December 2003 but many continued functioning under new names from different locations. However, the foreign terrorist component, largely Pakistani but with some Afghan elements, has now been essentially reduced to two principal formations, the Lashkar-e-Taiba (the militant limb of the Jamaat-ud Dawa) and the Jaish-e-Mohammad. Smaller formations remain.

Parts of J&K have been declared disturbed areas in which the Armed Forces Special Powers Act is applicable. The Army was long back redeployed along the LOC/international border, leaving the internal security cordons to be manned by para-military formations (such as the BSF, Rashtriya Rifles and CRPF) and, increasingly, the J&K Police. Cross-border infiltration has not stopped and random bombings, targeted killings and massacres continue.

The figures of casualties and arms seizures from 1990 to March 2006 tell their own horrific story.

The number of violent incidents (firings, grenade, bomb, IED and rocket attacks, arson, abductions, hangings, arms snatching) totalled over 64,200 against civilians and just under 29,600 against the security forces. There were hartals and demonstrations galore. Almost 16,000 civilians were killed and over 20,000 injured in militant/terrorist actions. The corresponding figures of JK Police and SF casualties were 4850 killed and over 11,650 injured.

The number of casualties suffered by militant/terrorist cadres was 20,816 killed. Over 37,100 surrendered and more than 17,800 were arrested. Of these, some 16,500 were released, on bail or were granted amnesty while 864 are in prison. Group clashes among militant/terrorist groups resulted in 650 fatalities and injuries to several others, including civilians caught in the crossfire.

Vast quantities of arms were seized during the same period, including over 28,250 AK-47/56/74 rifles, 10,225 pistols/revolvers, over a thousand universal machine guns, more than 1150 RPG, over 800 machine guns and sniper rifles and nearly 3450 rocket launchers/boosters. There was a correspondingly huge haul of ammunition and magazines.

Other seizures include over 1000 kg of RDX and almost 30,000 kg of other explosives, more than 5500 IEDs, nearly 6950 grenades and many thousands of mines, detonators and rockets, wireless sets and binoculars. Currency
recoveries from terrorists after 2001 alone amounted to Rs 2.24 crores in addition to lakhs of rupees in Pakistan, Afghan and fake currency.

Autonomy Debate

In 1996, President's Rule was lifted and elections were held despite dire threats, a boycott call and killings by armed militants. The National Conference under

Farooq Abdullah was returned on a platform demanding greater autonomy. Prime Minister Deve Gowda had promised "maximum autonomy" and Narasimha Rao had stated that "short of independence, the sky is the limit".

The new J&K Government accordingly set up an Autonomy Committee. Its terms of reference were to recommend measures for the restoration of the State's autonomy, necessary constitutional safeguards to render this arrangement inviolate, and "measures to ensure a harmonious relationship for the future between the State and the Union".

The State Autonomy Committee reported in April 1999 and recommended a return to the position that obtained in 1953, that is until the 1952 Agreement and whatever had been concluded before the arrest of Sheikh Abdullah in August 1953. But with regard to Part XII of the Indian Constitution, pertaining to finance, property, contracts and suits (Articles 264 to 300A), it noted as follows: "We are firmly of the opinion that in order that the State should be financially viable it needs more financial resources and assistance.... It is therefore recommended that the matter be discussed in depth between the State representatives and the Union Government".

Issues of regional autonomy within J&K have been a matter of periodic discussion and controversy and were variously addressed in the past by the Glancy,

Gajendragadkar and Sikri Commissions. Little was resolved and so this matter was entrusted to a new committee after the 1996 elections in order to satisfy regional aspirations and institute safeguards should J&K as a whole be vested with greater autonomy vis-à-vis the Centre. Jammu and sub-regions and distinctive communities within it, and both the Leh and Kargil districts of Ladakh have pleaded their concerns from time to time.

The Regional Autonomy Committee was divided but the report of the official group endorsed by three members was nonetheless presented in April 1999. This noted the ethno-cultural diversity of J&K and argued that autonomy should not result in new hegemonies. It accordingly recommended adoption of either of two options. The first proposed division of the State into eight new regions: three in the Valley, Doda plus (Chenab), Jammu, Rajouri-Poonch (Pir Panjal), Kargil and Ladakh. The alternative was to adopt the existing districts as units of devolution through a strengthened panchayati raj structure with agreed financial, linguistic and cultural safeguards.

The then NDA Government summarily rejected "autonomy" but said it was willing to discuss "devolution". However there has been a Leh Autonomous Development Council since 1996, which is working well, and a Kargil ADC followed in 2003.

Eight new districts were announced in J&K in the

summer of 2006 in the Jammu, Kashmir and Ladakh divisions. The announcement was well received as it makes for further devolution.

The Other Side of the Hill

Pakistan has divided the area of J&K administered by it into two parts, "Azad" J&K (PAK), and the Northern Areas.

(i) Pakistan Administered Jammu and Kashmir (PAK)

PAK has an area of 13,297 sq m and a population of 2.915 m (1998). An "Azad" Government was established on October 24, 1947 and functioned under Rules of Business framed by Pakistan from time to time until 1960 when a system of "basic democracies" was introduced. This was replaced in 1964 by an Azad J&K Act setting up an indirectly elected State Council, which underwent amendment in 1970 and again in 1974 (when the prevailing presidential system was replaced by a parliamentary system). The government was, however, suspended from 1977 to 1985 under an emergency decree promulgated by Islamabad.

The basic law of PAK remains the "Azad" J&K Interim Constitution of 1974, which saw eight amendments until November 1990. According to its Preamble, the Constitution was "approved" and its introduction "authorised" by the Government of Pakistan, which tells where power lies.

The oath at all levels, including that for civil servants, includes a commitment to "remain loyal to ...the cause of accession of the State of J&K to Pakistan". Article 7(2) of the Fundamental Rights chapter provides that "No person or political party ... shall be permitted to propagate against, or to take part in activities prejudicial or detrimental to, the ideology of the state's accession to Pakistan". The seven or eight pro-Independence parties that exist are systematically disqualified from contesting elections under this provision.

Shaukat Kashmiri, leader of the United Kashmir Peoples National Party has been living in exile in Geneva since 1999. Hamid Khan of the Balwaristan National Front is also compelled to live abroad.

Fundamental rights do not apply to actions by defence or other security forces responsible for public order. Freedom of speech is subject to reasonable restrictions in the interests of friendly relations with Pakistan!.

There is a 48 member Assembly and a nominated Council. The AJK or PAK Council is chaired by the Prime Minister of Pakistan and includes the PAK President, five nominees of the PM of Pakistan, the PM of PAK and six PAK MLAs. The Federal Minister for Kashmir Affairs and Northern Areas is an ex-officio Member. Although PAK has seven members on the Council as against six Federal representatives, Islamabad wields de facto power

The overriding power of the Council in relation to the Assembly is evident from the fact that Emergency powers vest in the Chairman (the Pakistan Prime Minister) who may order dissolution of the lower house. The Judges of the PAK Supreme Court and High Court, the Chief Election Commissioner and Auditor General are appointed on the advice of the Council. The Council's legislative powers extend to defence, foreign affairs, communication, currency and finance, corporations and the development of industries "in the public interest", planning, oil and natural gas, electricity, boilers, newspapers, books and printing presses, education, cinema exhibition, tourism, population planning and social welfare. PAK gets no royalty on hydro generation from the Mangla dam. This indicates that the media and education are under direct federal control.

The Chief Secretary, IG Police, Accountant General and Finance Secretary of PAK are appointees of Islamabad.

Even as General Musharraf talks of "self-rule", things have not changed in PAK. The general elections held there in July 2006 represents another charade with the disqualification of some 81 candidates unwilling to swear by "the ideology of accession to Pakistan", including those belonging to Amanullah's Khan's JKLF.

Further, 12 members of the 41 member legislature were "elected" from the so-called J&K diaspora (refugees) in Pakistan, a pocket borough of the ISI. With six women members being elected by the House, there is as always a safe majority to root for Pakistan while the Ministry of Kashmir Affairs and Northern Areas (KANA) rules the roost.

(ii) The Northern Areas

The Northern Areas is spread over 72,495 sq kms and has a population of 0.8 m (1994), though some estimates place it around 1.5 m. It has been described as a "colony" of Pakistan with a pretence of recently upgraded powers that does not vest it with much autonomy. It is something of an out of bounds strategic region and is administered virtually directly by Islamabad. It was severed from PAK in 1949, is not a province of Pakistan and enjoys minimal democratic rights.

The majority Shia (Baltistan and Nagar), Aga Khani or Ismaili (Gilgit, Hunza, Ishkoman, Punial, Yasin, Gupis) and scattered Nurbakshi (sufi) population has been subject to discriminatory pressure, and there is evidence of demographic change through Sunni in-migration of traders and security personnel. Shia-Sunni riots have been endemic and Gilgit was under curfew through much of 2005.

In a suit filed by certain petitioners in 1990 before the

High Court of PAK, it was argued that the Northern Areas was part of PAK and must be restored to it. The plea was strongly supported by the PAK Government, which stated that the Northern Areas lacked basic human rights under Pakistan. The High Court upheld the complaint and an appeal by the Pakistan Government was turned down by the PAK Supreme Court. The Pakistan Government thereupon referred the matter to the Supreme Court of Pakistan. Its ruling was that the Northern Areas was indeed part of PAK but it nevertheless struck down the plaint as infructuous on the technical ground that the Northern Areas was not under Muzaffarabad's administrative control at the time.

The Northern Areas continues to suffer from several limitations on freedom of speech, assembly, movement and conscience.

A Northern Areas Advisory Council was formed in 1970 with 14 members. This was successively upgraded to a NA Council and then, following a Pakistan Supreme Court Order, to a NA Legislative Council. Apparently no legislation was adopted between 1999 and 2004 but 18 Resolutions were adopted all of which were reportedly ignored by the all-powerful Kashmir Affairs and Northern Areas (KANA) Ministry in Islamabad. The NALC membership has now been increased from 24 to 36 with the addition of six so-called technocrat members and six women. Elections to these seats were held on March 22, 2006.

The NA movement for real autonomy or provincial status continues. In May 2004,the Gilgit-Baltistan Thinkers Forum and All-Parties National Alliance (APNA) appealed to the Pakistan Supreme Court to expedite hearings on a 1999 petition seeking grant of fundamental rights to the people of NA on par with citizens of Pakistan. The matter is still pending.

Siachen, "Thence North to the Glaciers"

The Cease Fire Line (CFL), a military line, was in 1972 designated the Line of Control (LOC), notionally a political line in keeping with the terms of the Simla Agreement.

However, after its boundary agreement with China in 1963, Pakistan had begun to develop its line of communications east of Skardu and, still later, commenced licensing mountaineering expeditions desirous of climbing in the High Karakoram east of K2 and exploring the mighty glaciers that characterise the region. Then, sometime after 1967, the US Defence Mapping Agency gratuitously redefined the Line beyond NJ 9842, aligning the LOC not north to the glaciers but northeast to the international boundary just short of the Karakoram Pass. A charitable explanation could be that the dotted air defence information zone (ADIZ) marking in military aeronautical maps was mistakenly hardened to depict the extended LOC beyond NJ 9842. Pakistan in due course adopted the same definition of the extended

LOC and changed its maps accordingly, as did several world atlases. This was cartographic aggression. The US has been sheepish and never been able to explain the gaffe.

If a line is drawn due "north to the glaciers" from NJ 9842 to the international boundary, the Siachen snout, from which the Nubra River issues, and the greater part of the glacier, that extends 75 km north-northwest of this point, will be seen to fall on the Indian side of the LOC. Getting wind that Pakistan had readied plans to occupy Siachen, India pre-empted any such move by occupying the glacier right up to its northern extremity, Indra Col, in April 1984.

India's Actual Ground Position Line (AGPL), beyond NJ 9842, has since run along the Saltoro Ridge that marks the western wall of the Siachen glacier. The glacier protects the northern approaches to Leh but is otherwise of little strategic value.

In the last round of Indo-Pak negotiations on Siachen (May 2006), the Indian side reiterated its insistence on authentication by Pakistan of the AGPL from which both sides may pull back under an agreed redeployment arrangement. This, however, would leave untouched the basic issue of where the extended LOC ran beyond NJ 9842 prior to India's positioning itself on the present AGPL in 1984. Pakistan was not there. Nor could it have been a no-man's land under the Karachi/Suchetgarh Agreements.

Therefore, unless the LOC is drawn as required from (NJ 9842) "thence north to the glaciers", India will be redrawing (its) boundaries in contravention of Dr Manmohan Singh's firm declaration that boundaries cannot (will not) be redrawn, thus making nonsense of its negotiating position and risking a new situation that causes the LOC to unravel.

Pakistan's Case on J&K

Pakistan bases its right to J&K, and more especially the Vale of Kashmir and adjacent tracts on the ideological basis of its Islamic affiliation. Kashmir is also said to represent the "K" in the Pakistan acronym. Thus the reference to J&K being "the unfinished business of Partition". Apart from being contiguous with Pakistan, the argument is that it offers it strategic depth, provides overland access to China and encompasses the upper catchment of the Indus, which constitutes Pakistan's lifeline.

The religious argument is specious. There are over 140 million Muslims in India or nearly as many as in Pakistan. In 1947 a referendum was held in the NWFP, a 98 per cent Muslim majority province, to determine its future status as it had until then been governed by an elected Congress government before being placed under Governor's rule. Likewise, the Chittagong Hill Tracts, with a mere two per cent Muslim population, was allotted to (East) Pakistan though contiguous to

India. In any event, Pakistan wanted the Princely States to be kept outside the main Partition settlement.

The "lifeline" argument was conclusively laid to rest with the Indus Waters Treaty in 1990. This safeguards Pakistan's position and is the one Indo-Pakistan agreement that has survived wars and confrontation, despite recent controversies.

Much is made of Radcliffe awarding some parts of Gurdaspur district to India that gave it easier connectivity with J&K. The Himachal states that had acceded to India provided contiguity and connectivity too. But the reason for awarding the two Gurdaspur tehsils in question to India was to ensure that Amritsar was not detached from East Punjab - a proposition that the Sikhs would have resisted - especially with a tongue of Kapurthala, a yet-to-accede Princely state, intervening in between. This illustrates the weightage given by Radcliffe to "other factors" under his terms of reference, other examples being the award of the Chittagong Hill Tracts to Pakistan, so as not to rob Chittagong Port of its hinterland, and the Nadia rivers to whomsoever got Calcutta.

If anybody violated the contiguity principal it was Pakistan, which intrigued with Junagadh, Hyderabad, Jodhpur, Jaisalmer, Travancore and other princely states, seeking to detach them from India. Even as late as 1969, Zulfikar Ali Bhutto wrote of a "truncated", moth eaten Pakistan without Assam, Tripura and much else. (See his "The Myth of Independence". OUP, London, 1969).

If Pakistan denounces Maharaja Hari Singh's accession to India as a fraud and argues that he fled from the State, leaving Srinagar, it ignores the huge beam in its own eye on matters of accession. In removing to Jammu, his winter capital, the Maharaja did not flee the State, which had been invaded by Pakistan. However it was the Muslim League that vehemently insisted that with the lapse of paramountcy the Princes would regain sovereignty and that therefore the word of the ruler must be final. It was the Congress that argued that in case of any doubt, the popular will should be ascertained. It was on this basis that while accepting J&K's accession, Nehru volunteered reference to the people once its soil had been cleared of the invader, normalcy restored and those displaced had returned to their homes and avocations. Those conditions were never fulfilled.

Independence and Mediation

Some, like the JKLF, plead for J&K's independence. The fact is that J&K was virtually independent between August 15 and October 26, 1947. That independence was rudely extinguished by Pakistan, which had even earlier sought to strangulate J&K by choking off essential supplies and services despite having signed a Standstill Agreement.

As for mediation, the UN itself mediated directly and through designated UN Representatives from 1948 until 1958. Thereafter there was mediation in 1963 by the US-UK duo, Averell Harriman and Duncan Sandys, by the Russians in 1965-66 and various other individuals and groups more informally thereafter.

In some cases self-styled mediators have been part of the problem, especially the cold warriors of yore.

Human Rights, Alienation and Reconciliation

There have undoubtedly been gross human rights violations in J&K– encounter killings, torture, custodial deaths, cordon-and-search operations, continuous curfews, brutalities and harassment, disappearances, rape, arson, extortion, executions, hartals and disruption – on all sides, by the security forces and agents of the State as well as by various non-state actors, local and foreign.

Violations by the State and its agents have shown a distinct downward trend despite continuing lapses from time to time. There is no immunity and impunity as alleged by some as the Indian media, human rights groups, political parties, courts and civil society have exercised vigilance.

In the context of insurgency, armed militant groups and their cross-border patrons have also been prone to use human rights violations, real or imagined, as weapons in waging war for the hearts and minds of the populace. Well-known international human rights agencies and elements of the foreign media fell into this trap, especially during the initial years. Many, including governments, are wiser today.

The notion that rape and other human rights violations by members of the security forces go unpunished is unfounded as the following figures of Army courts martial and action taken from 1990 to April 2006 indicate:

The complaints filed against Army personnel numbered 890 of which 854 were investigated, the rest being under investigation. As many as 830 allegations were found to be baseless and only 24 were proven. Based on these findings, 47 personnel were punished for causing death (two), rape (six), molestation (eight), and theft, extortion, injuries to civilians or militants (eight). In six cases cash compensation was awarded to the victims. The sentences awarded against those found guilty included rigorous imprisonment for varying periods, dismissal, etcetera.

The para-military forces have their own disciplinary mechanisms.

Nevertheless, India needs to do much more to heal the wounds, ameliorate trauma, reverse the sense of alienation that resides in many hearts and make all sections of the people of J&K feel at all times that they are equal citizens of a truly plural and secular society. There is a trust and democratic deficit in J&K that must be overcome.

The Pandits must be encouraged to return to their homeland and be rehabilitated in safety and with dignity and honour. Those trapped across the LOC as refugees or who were inveigled across the divide as "freedom fighters" and have come to recognise the error of their ways must also be enabled to return. An amnesty should be available for those against whom there are no charges of heinous crime. There has to be an exit from the sorry past, with much to forgive and forget on all sides in a spirit of reconciliation and trust. Yet, those against whom clear charges of human rights violation lie, must be brought to book as peace and justice go hand in hand.

The Hurriyat

The Simla Accord of 1972 produced many years of peace though not a J&K settlement. India was remiss in not moving more actively on this front but was let down by Zufikar Ali Bhutto who had agreed that "the Line (of Control) could be gradually endowed with the characteristics of an international border". (See P. N. Dhar, Times of India, November 1995). The Soviet intervention in Afghanistan spurred US efforts to overthrow the "evil empire" This made Pakistan a frontline state. US support and Zia-ul Haq's Islamisation drive, combined to make Pakistan a school for radical Islam and the training of jihadis and terrorists (who fanned out worldwide, not least into J&K), an arms bazaar and hub for drug running and proliferation. The notorious Dr A.Q. Khan ran what has been dubbed a nuclear Walmart – obviously with official approval and support.

Siachen (post-1984) and the rise of militancy in J&K after 1989 saw Indo-Pakistan relations plummet, with an intensification of violence in J&K. The All Party Hurriyat Conference (APHC) was formed, a disparate grouping of some 34 associations with a core of seven political parties. They espoused different ideologies, tendencies, membership, patrons and ambitions ranging from independence for J&K to accession to Pakistan to varying degrees of partition and greater autonomy. The differences have sometimes been acute, leading to internecine violence and killings. The former Mir Waiz was gunned down in 1990 by suspected Hizb militants and Abdul Ghani Lone of the Peoples Conference more recently by pro-Pakistan elements. Most, if not all of the major Hurriyat leaders have enjoyed or continue to enjoy security protection from the Indian state, which they are loath to lose for fear of their own friends. The cost to the State of providing security to APHC leaders during 2004 and 2005 was over Rs 1.16 crores, accordingly to an official statement. The beneficiaries included Mir Waiz Umar Farooq, Prof Abdul Ghani Bhatt, Moulvi Abbas Ansari, Shabir Ahmad Shah and others.

Some of those earlier underground have, however, come overground and are boldly waging a battle for peace. They have realised that violence offers no solution.

The Hurriyat has boycotted polls in J&K since 1996. It has travelled the world and insisted on meeting President Musharraf regularly but has been chary of revealing its hand other than calling for Kashmiris to be represented in any negotiations and claiming an exclusive place at the table for itself. Moulvi Umar Farooq, the new Mir Waiz, has recently mooted the idea of a United States of J&K whereas Syed Ali Shah Geelani, the breakaway Jamaat-e-Islami leader, is on record as stating that the J&K question is not territorial but religious. The Hurriyat can yet play a constructive role in the peace process but cannot claim a veto.

Peace Process

Mr Inder Gujral and Mr Nawaz Sharif held a series of meetings through 1997 when officials of the two sides identified several topics for formal discussion. Nuclear tests by India followed by Pakistan in May 1998 interrupted the process, which was resumed when Mr Atal Behari Vaypayee visited Pakistan in February 1999 and signed the Lahore Agreement with Mr Nawaz Sharif.

Unknown to India, the Pakistan Army had by then already initiated the military infiltration across the LOC that led to the Kargil War in the summer of 1999. (See "From Surprise to Reckoning: The Kargil Review Committee Report. Sage, 2000). The pretence that this was a J&K "mujahideen" strike from the Indian side in a sector where the LOC was fuzzy scarcely afforded a fig-leaf in those icy heights. The deception, subterfuge and efforts at maintaining secrecy stood fully exposed and self-confessed with the interception of telephonic conversations between Lt. General Mohammad Aziz, the Pakistan Army Chief of General Staff in Rawalpindi and the Army Chief, General Pervez Musharraf, then visiting Beijing on May 26 and 29, 1999. (See Text of the intercepts by R&AW reproduced in Jaswant Singh's "A Call to Honour". Rupa, Delhi, 2006). The Musharraf tapes were released to the world contemporaneously by the Indian Government and was further corroborated with many more details by documents and other material captured by the Indian Army during the Kargil campaign. (Annexures to the Kargil Review Committee Report. Government of India, New Delhi, 2000).

Pakistan's gambit failed miserably and a coup led to Nawaz Sharif's ouster and General Musharraf's assumption of office as President, wearing his uniform, under a new Legal Framework Order that subsequently saw the military constitutionally entrenched as a limb of government and final arbiter through the mechanism of a National Security Council. (See "Ghaddar Kaun" a biography in Urdu of Nawaz Sharif by Suhail Warraich of Geo-TV and Jang, Lahore.

2006. Also see Pakistan Muslim League's "White Paper on Kargil". Islamabad, 2006).

Despite General Musharraf's virulent denunciation of the Lahore process, Mr Vajpayee invited him for talks at Agra in the summer of 2000, where avoidable grandstanding on the part of the visiting President led to an impasse. The events of 9/11 brought about a sea change, initially perhaps tactical then increasingly strategic, in Pakistan's posture under US pressure. Islamabad agreed to join the war on terror, end support for the Taliban and dismantle the terrorist infrastructure in place in aid of cross-border jihadi elements.

President Musharraf has since taken some bold measures despite three attempts on his life from right wing extremists. Both sides agreed on a ceasefire along the LOC on November 26, 2003. This has provided considerable relief and given impetus to the peace process. Nevertheless, India has insisted that there cannot be good terrorists (so-called "freedom fighters") and bad terrorists and that Pakistan must act on its repeated promises to ban terrorist groups engaged in J&K and other parts of India, desist from cross-border activity and dismantle the jihadi infrastructure. It must also pursue the composite dialogue as a whole and not make CBMs and agreement on other issues hostage to what it decrees to be progress on Kashmir.

The agreement on starting a Srinagar-Muzaffarabad bus service for divided families in J&K using simple travel documents signals new hope. Similar bus services on other routes in J&K such as Poonch-Rawalakote and Jammu-Sialkot are due to start and trucks are also to be permitted to ply, initiating trade across the LOC. Unfortunately the earthquake intervened, putting back the schedule for additional connectivity. Talks on other issues like Siachen, the Wular Barrage and various CBMs are inching forward, but Pakistan remains reluctant to permit movement between Kargil and Skardu.

The Great Earthquake

The Great J&K Earthquake of October 8, 2005 along the LOC caused huge devastation, especially on the Pakistan side, with its epicentre north of Muzaffarabad. When the dust settled, reportedly as many as 17 jihadi groups, either banned by Pakistan or on its terrorism watch list, were found to have crawled out of the rubble, using pseudonyms or operating as front organisations. Despite having taken casualties, they were active in providing relief and rehabilitation along the LOC within PAK.

The Pakistan Army scrambled to reinforce and repair its battered defence line along the LOC and only thereafter came forward to take charge of relief operations. The jihadis, Pakistan NGOs and international relief agencies came in earlier and remain in the forefront. The PAK Government and leadership have been conspicuously absent on the ground or even in the media, exposing their irrelevance.

Jihadi Future: A Riddle Wrapped in an Enigma

The role and future of the jihadi elements remains a riddle. They have resurfaced despite bans and are now partnering on-going relief and rehabilitation programmes, gaining respectability and staging a come back. The only way for Pakistan to purge itself is to go the whole way in clearing its soil and society of the jihadi culture.

The world has seen through Pakistan's Kashmir veil. "Pakistan's Kashmir policy has become a huge burden... Every terrorist attack that now occurs in either India or Pakistan clarifies that the "core issue" on the sub-continent has become terrorism, not Kashmir. And because of Pakistan's choice of a Kashmir policy that relies so heavily on proxy violence to leverage India, Islamabad has lost the presumption of innocence whenever horrific acts of well-coordinated terror are directed against India...".(Michael Krepon, "The Meaning of the Mumbai Blasts". Stimson Centre, Washington, D.C. August 7, 2006).

Fortunately, some in Pakistan too have, even if fitfully, begun to realise the need to chart a new course on

Kashmir and relations with India, whether out of conviction or enlightened self-interest. Pakistan's Education Minister and former ISI Chief, Javed Ashraf Qazi was reported on March 6, 2004 as stating: " We must not be afraid of admitting that Jaish-e-Mohammad was involved in the deaths of thousands of innocent Kashmiris, in the bombing of the Indian Parliament, in Daniel Pearl's murder and in attempts on General Pervez Musharraf's life and that both Jaish (JeM) and Lashkar (LeT) have harmed the Kashmir struggle the most". (Daily Times, Islamabad, March 6 and 7, 2004).

Despite such statements, cross border strikes and bombings continue in J&K and other parts of India. Pakistan persists in asking India for more and yet more evidence of culpability and has yet to act on Delhi's demand that it hand over a given list of hard core terrorists charged with criminal activity in India. These men still operate against India from and through Pakistan and enjoy official patronage.

Manmohan's Road Map

Pakistan keeps saying that it is anxious to move the Peace Process forward far more rapidly and President Musharraf has himself been tireless in making a variety of suggestions about what India must do. Dr Manmohan Singh, however, has set out a framework for sustained progress, step by step, without any further partitioning of India. Speaking at Amritsar on

March 24, 2006 he reiterated that boundaries cannot be redrawn, "but we can work towards making them irrelevant ...just lines on a map". In his view, other issues that divide India and Pakistan cannot also be made hostage to progress on J&K as progress on any one issue will create a more favourable environment for the resolution of all other issues, especially more prickly ones like J&K.

The Prime Minister suggested that "both sides begin a dialogue with the people in their areas of control to improve the quality of governance so as to give people on both sides a greater chance of leading a life of dignity and self-respect". He envisioned a "common cooperative future" for the two parts of J&K as well as India and Pakistan, with "consultative mechanisms ... to maximise the gains of cooperation in solving problems of social and economic development in the region".

He set out this vision in the broader framework of effective Indo-Pakistan cooperative strategies to give concrete shape to this shared vision. He urged Pakistan to accept ground realities and look at the future. He envisaged both sides working together to open up new opportunities of economic cooperation not only in South Asia but in West and Central Asia and he saw the peace process culminating in a Treaty of Peace, Security and Friendship.

This is a profoundly significant statement. It calls on

the two sides in J&K jointly to work towards internal self-determination, with maximum internal autonomy on either side. Yet each side will remain part of India and Pakistan respectively and could yet be bound together by overarching mechanisms that evolve for mutual cooperation and consultation, straddling the present LOC.

Pakistan cannot get at the peace table what is has been unable to win on the battlefield or through years of proxy war. The Manmohan Singh road map offers Islamabad an honourable settlement in J&K with an indirect stake in the Indian part of the State and legitimisation of its control over what should also become a truly autonomous PAK and Northern Areas in which India will have a similar indirect stake.

Current Status

A process for negotiating an internal resolution in J&K has been set in motion with the Round Table Conference of all parties and stakeholders that Dr Manmohan Singh convened in Delhi in March 2006. It was boycotted by the Hurriyat group, which again boycotted the second RTC on May 24-25 in Srinagar on the ground that it did not wish to be part of a "crowd", most of whose members had no basic quarrel with Delhi. However, the door has been held open for it to join any time in the future. Should it choose to remain apart, it will become increasingly irrelevant. None can have a veto on the peace process. The jihadis have, as before, greeted the RTC with murderous attacks on innocents.

The Srinagar RTC ended with an agreement to constitute a credible mechanism for more intimate and detailed deliberations to (i) build consensus on CBMs across segments of society in J&K including bringing back the Pandits; (ii) strengthen relations across the LOC through trade, tourism and pilgrimage; (iii) promote economic development; (iv) ensure good governance, including zero tolerance for human rights violations, transparency and accountability, and strengthen local self-government; and (v) build centre-state and intra-regional relations through greater autonomy/devolution to and within J&K.

Many elements fear peace and have a vested interest in continuing insurgency and unrest. There will be determined spoilers and violent efforts by the jihadis and their mentors to disrupt the process. But India must persevere.

Meanwhile, major developments are afoot. Construction of the Udhamapur- Baramulla Railway is proceeding apace both in the Hill section and in the Valley. The line should be fully operational by 2008-09, and earlier in the Valley. This will have a transforming effect, taken with the completion around the same time of a new all-weather North-South Highway linking Jammu with Srinagar along a new and shorter alignment that will pierce the Pir Panjal at a lower altitude than the present Bannihal tunnel. Srinagar is soon to become an international airport and the commissioning of new hydro projects and transmission lines will turn around the energy situation in the State.

Taken together, these offer opportunity to unveil a medium and longer term vision of peace and development giving strong impetus to domestic and foreign investment and employment and income generation in the State.

Indus-II

J&K believes that it got a raw deal from the Indus Waters Treaty as it was deprived of its legitimate share of this natural resource. This is a mistaken view. India secured the entire waters of the three Eastern rivers, the Sutlej, Beas and Ravi, which do not flow through J&K (barring some minor influents of the Ravi), and specified uses for J&K from the three Western Rivers, the Chenab, Jhelum and Indus, which were otherwise allocated in their entirety to Pakistan.

All existing water uses in J&K as of 1960 were protected under the Treaty. Over and beyond that India is permitted 1.34 m acres of additional irrigation in the State, against which only 642,477 acres had actually been brought under irrigation by 2005. Further, India is permitted 3.60 MAF of storage on the Western

Rivers, primarily on the Chenab and Jhelum, categorised sector-wise under general conservation, power and flood storage and by main rivers and their tributaries. J&K is well below the ceiling in every segment and has built practically no "storages" as against run-of-river "pondages" as at Sallal, Dul Hasti and Baglihar on the Chenab and Uri on the Jhelum. Pakistan has challenged the Baglihar project, which has been referred to a Swiss Neutral Expert under the Indus Water Treaty to adjudicate the "difference".

Pakistan is currently raising the height of the Mangla dam on the Jhelum by 30 feet, in view of siltation, to store an additional 2.88 MAF of water by 2008. Its proposal to build the Basha-Diamer storage dam on the Indus in the Northern Areas (950 feet high, 7.34 MAF, 4500 MW), costing $6.7 bn (2004) has been questioned by India. This will take seven years to construct and also entail upgrading and widening the Karakoram Highway from Manshera to Chilas.

An even larger mega-dam has been studied by Pakistan at Skardu-Katzarah (35,000 MAF, 15,000 MW). But this will drown Skardu and Balti cultural sites and strategic roads and is therefore strongly opposed. Both the proposed Basha-Diamer and Skardu-Katzarah dams are entirely snow fed and conceived of as "carry over" storages that may only fill once in five to eight years.

Pakistan faces increasing water stress and has few storage sites on the Indus system, the headwaters of the three Western Rivers being controlled by India. Pakistan's free use of the Kabul river thus far is now being challenged by Afghanistan, which needs to develop its own water resources. India, on the other hand, has Treaty limitations on its harnessing and exploitation of the waters of the Western rivers, especially the Indus. With clear evidence of climate change and receding glaciers, it is estimated by a World Bank consultant that the lean season flow of the Indus may diminish by 30 per cent over the next 30 years.

These trends will affect Northwest India and Pakistan equally as both are dependent on the Indus system. Article VII of the Indus Treaty on Future Cooperation speaks of a "common interest in the optimum development of the (Indus) Rivers". It accordingly enjoins the two sides "to cooperate, by mutual consent, to the fullest possible extent... in undertaking engineering works in the Rivers". The time has come for such cooperation not only on account of climate change but also to reinforce the Peace Process in J&K, which would be powerfully underpinned by any such initiative. Joint site surveys and appropriate geological, hydrological, glacier, meteorological, sediment, seismic and other environmental studies could be undertaken throughout J&K, not least in Ladakh and the Northern Areas to establish the possibilities and potentials. Existing dams could also be raised or redesigned wherever possible to enhance storage. This by itself would make boundaries irrelevant in J&K and pave the way for a whole range of cooperative endeavours and cross-border institution-building in all of J&K. This arrangement would not undermine the Indus Treaty, but build on it.

Such an initiative would be well timed immediately after the receipt of the Neutral Expert's report on Baglihar that is expected in November 2006, whatever the verdict.

Karakoram Peace Park

A Siachen accord on the withdrawal of security forces from either side to agreed redeployment positions is under negotiation. However, Pakistan needs to correct its maps depicting the extended LOC beyond NJ 9842. Once this is done, the entire glaciated region in the "V" between NJ 9842, K2 and the terminal point of Pakistan's claim line just west of the Karakoram Pass could be made a demilitarised zone of peace and an international High Karakoram Peace Park, which China could be invited to join by bringing the Shaksgam Valley into its ambit.

The Park could be made available for scientific exploration, climate change monitoring and mountaineering and trekking expeditions. Its base, around NJ 9842 could be made a High Karakoram Base Station for proposed Indus-II studies.

From SAARC to Asian Community

It is not without significance that the threads of post-Agra Indo-Pakistan diplomacy were picked up at the Islamabad SAARC summit in 2003. The meeting endorsed the vision of a South Asian Free Trade Area (SAFTA) leading to a South Asian Community by 2020. This is an old dream, earlier aborted, that can be realised. A J&K settlement within a Indo-Pakistan Accord, within the larger framework of a South Asian Community linked to China and ASEAN in the east and to Afghanistan, Iran and West Asia in the West would conform to the larger unfolding vision of an Asian Community to which Dr Manmohan Singh and President Musharraf have separately alluded, each in his own way.

Working together, India and Pakistan can do so much to uplift their own people and regenerate South Asia and the wider neighbourhood in the interests of global peace and prosperity. Despite everything, the hope underlying Partition on both sides, traumatic and painful though it was, was that this was a separation of states but not of people. They would sooner rather than later come together, secure in their respective countries, as friends and neighbours linked by bonds of a shared history, geography and culture.

The time has come to make that hope a living reality. The Indian "threat" has militarised Pakistan and entrenched the Pakistan Army as the country's principal power-centre in alliance with feudal elements and the religious right at the cost of democracy and social change. Yet Pakistan is essentially a liberal Islamic society influenced by the sufi tradition, as is Bangladesh and India. Together, South Asia, representing 40 per cent of the Islamic world, could help rescue World Islam from the sense of despair and helplessness that assails it in West and Central Asia and North Africa.

A Moment of Truth ?

Critics are beginning to see Kashmir not as the "core issue" – for whom ? – but as a red herring. As the PPP leader, Ms Benazir Bhutto said (July 2006), it provides the raison d'etre for the Army and ISI to enjoy unaccountable power and pelf. More deeply, the Kashmir slogan has served as a rallying point that binds Pakistan in the absence of a more positive idea than a crude rejection of "Hindu India".

This, however, begs the question that not many Pakistanis have dared ask themselves. What is Pakistan? Fifty-eight years after independence it remains unsure about its civilisation, history, constitution, major institutions, federalism, citizenship and future. It exemplifies a proud and talented people in search of a state and a state in search of its soul, driven by negatives and unable to rise above defining itself as "the other", the battle for Pakistan having scarcely been joined in Punjab, the Frontier, Baluchistan or even Sind. It was essentially waged and won in what is today's India. Tragically, much innocent blood was shed on both sides; but that nothwithstanding, the idea of Pakistan has remained enigmatic.

Jinnah envisaged a modern, liberal, democratic, secular Pakistan, a co-sharer of united India's heritage, as testified by his August 11, 1947 inaugural address before Pakistan's constituent assembly. Sadly, he died too soon. So did Liaqat Ali, shortly thereafter, trapping Pakistan in a cycle of feudal-military alternation, with Kashmir and, now, radical Islam sustaining a vaguely conceived "ideology of Pakistan" reflected in its officially sponsored school textbooks critically analysed by a group of independent Pakistani scholars a few year ago. ("The Subtle Subversion: The State of Curricula and Textbooks in Pakistan". Compiled by A.H. Nayyar and Ahmed Salim. The Sustainable Development Policy Institute, Pakistan, Islamabad, 2003). India too is endangered by revivalist tendencies, but its democratic roots and traditions are, hopefully, stronger.

It does not serve India to have a weak, troubled, fractured Pakistan. It is therefore in its highest interest, while standing firm, patiently to lead Islamabad towards an honourable and principled settlement such as Dr Manmohan Singh has envisioned. Sooner than later, Pakistan will discover its soul and find fulfilment in a just resolution of its perceived disputes with India. That day need not be too far away.

Bombay Blasts

Tragically, the murderous Bombay blasts in July 2006 that took a toll of over 185 lives have, following on the great earthquake, caused another set-back to Indo-Pakistan relations, this time, manmade. The level of violence and targeted communal killings by terrorists had gone up in Kashmir and countrywide even earlier. Rash alternatives such as retaliatory strikes and hot pursuit have fortunately not found favour, despite perfervid cries of "appeasement" from the India's Hindu right extreme, which only echoes and justifies the voices of jihadi fundamentalism in Pakistan. However, the blasts have given pause to the peace process, rather than its abandonment, while the future course of action is reviewed in all its aspects.

Conclusion

The dialogue must go forward. Kashmir is not the core issue. It is both the cause and consequence of the souring of Indo-Pakistan relations. Be that as it may, it is time to move on from confrontation to reconciliation.

India needs to build itself and play its role as a mature, emerging power without the debilitating distraction of trying to counter Pakistan at all times and at all levels. It needs to put the hurt and trauma of Partition behind it and steer South Asia forward as a bulwark of democracy, stability, peace and cooperation in a troubled world.

Many in Pakistan ask what it gains after sacrificing so much blood and treasure over J&K when a settlement along the LOC or more could have been had decades ago. The answer is that what it has on offer today, if it travels Manmohan Singh's road map, is more than anything previously conceived, even as it legitimises its presence in PAK and the Northern Areas. Indeed both sides stand to gain an indirect stake in the other part of J&K. The peace dividend would be of immense emotional, security and material benefit to both sides. Most of all to the people of Jammu and Kashmir for whom the Line of Control would have become a bridge.

The object of this Primer is not to score debating points but to present facts starkly in the interests of an honourable solution. Nor, as mentioned before, is it intended to be a complete or detailed history. Many events are missing. The effort has been to demolish myths and put things in context so that India and Pakistan, together with the people of J&K on both sides of the LOC, are able to redeem the past by what they collectively make of the future.

It has truly been said that Peace hath its victories no less renowned than War.

Appendix

List of J&K/India related militant organisations/tanzeems

J&K Liberation Front.(1964) Aim, an independent and united J&K. The Indian faction, led by Yasin Malik, declared a ceasefire in 1994. The Pakistan faction is headed by Amanullah Khan who lives in Islamabad.

People's League, led by Shabir Shah.

Hizb-ul-Mujahideen (HM). Led by Syed Salahuddin, now in Muzaffarabad. Its objective is accession to Pakistan. Sponsored by the ISI in 1989 to counter the JKLF and wean away some of its disgruntled cadres some of whom reappeared as:

Al Badr, initially founded in 1989, but regrouped in 1998 with foreign cadres. Headed by Bakht Zamin.

Al Umar, 1990.

Ihkwan-ul-Muslimeen, created from the terrorist wing of the J&K Students League in 1991.

Dukhtarran-e-Millat (Daughters of the Nation), an Islamist women's group and moral censor(1987). Headed by Aasiya Andrabi.

Allah Tigers

Hizb-ul Nisa

Mutahida Jihad Council, a Muzaffarabad based body formed in 1991 for overall coordination.

All Parties Hurriyat Conference (APHC), a political front of several organisations. This has divided. The moderate wing is led by the Mir Waiz, Maulana Umar Farooq and the radical, pro-Pakistan wing by Syed Ali Shah Geelani. Both factions operate from Srinagar.

Harkat-ul Ansar, 1993. General Secretary, Maulana Masood Azhar, who was arrested in February 1994 but released in exchange for the hi-jacked IC 814 airline passengers in Kandahar in December 1999. This later became the **Harkat-ul Mujahideen**, which later used Al Faran as a front organisation.

Harkat ul-Jihad-al-Islami, 1997.

Lashkar-e-Taiba (LeT), founded by Hafeez Saeed and built up by the ISI with the decline of the HUA in 1993.

J&K Students Liberation Front, 2000 (renamed Khuddamul Islam) operates the

Al-Rahman Trust in PAK for earthquake relief.
Jamaat-e-Furqan a splinter group of JeM has resurfaced in PAK as the **Al-Asr Trust** for purposes of earthquake relief.
Muslim Janbaz Force (May 1990) formed under Babar Badr.
Kashmir Jihad Force
Al Jihad Force
Jamait ul-Mujahideen (JuM).
Lashkar-e Jabbar (LeJ).
Al Barq
Tehrik-e Mujahideen, under Sheikh Jamilur Rehman.
J&K National Federation Army
Mahaz-e Azadi
Islami Jihad-e Tulba
Tehrik-e Hurriyat-e-Kashmir
Tehrik e-Nifaz-e-Fiwqar Jafaria
Al Mustafa Liberation Fighters
Tehrik-e-Islam-e-Jihadi
Muslim Mujahideen
Tehrik-Jihad
Islam Inquilabi Mahaz
Hizbul Tehrik
Tehrik Nifaz-e-Shariat Muhammadi
Jamaat-e-Daawa (JuD) headed by Hafiz Saeed , formed after the LeT was nominally banned by the Pakistan authorities in 2002. Was involved in earthquake relief in PAK after October 2005.

Note:

The ISI has preferred fragmentation, in order better to control these tanzeems which it has trained, armed, financed and otherwise assisted over the years. The linkages between them are of Byzantine complexity and they have kept fading and reappearing under new identities from time to time, partly as a cover to establish plausible deniability.

Many of these tanzeems are/were primarily made up of "guest mujahideen" drawn from PAK, Pakistan proper, Afghanistan and even further afield. The Afghanistan-J&K nexus has been well established.

Several militants have surrendered and resumed normal life. Some have joined the peace process. One prominent leader, Kukka Parrey, came overground and joined the counter-insurgency movement until gunned down some years later.

(Compiled from data obtained by kind courtesy of the Institute of Conflict Management, Delhi, and its website www.south asian terrorism portal, and sundry other sources).

Select Bibliography

- Kashmir: A Study in Indo-Pakistan Relations by Sisir Gupta. Asia Publishing House, Bombay, 1966
- The Kashmir Story, B.L. Sharma. Asia Publishing House, 1967
- A History of Kashmir, P.N.K Bamzai, Metropolitan Book Co, Delhi. 1962
- Essential Documents and Notes on the Kashmir Dispute, P.L. Lakhanpal, International Publications, New Delhi, 1958
- The Constitution of J&K, Its Development and Comments, A.S. Anand. Universal Book Traders, Delhi, 1980
- Report of the State Autonomy Committee, Jammu, April 1999
- Regional Autonomy Committee Report, April 1999
- The Transfer of Power 1942-47, Constitutional Relations between Britain and India. Editor Nicholas Mansergh, Vols 1-12, HMSO, London, 1970-83.

Notes

Notes

Und

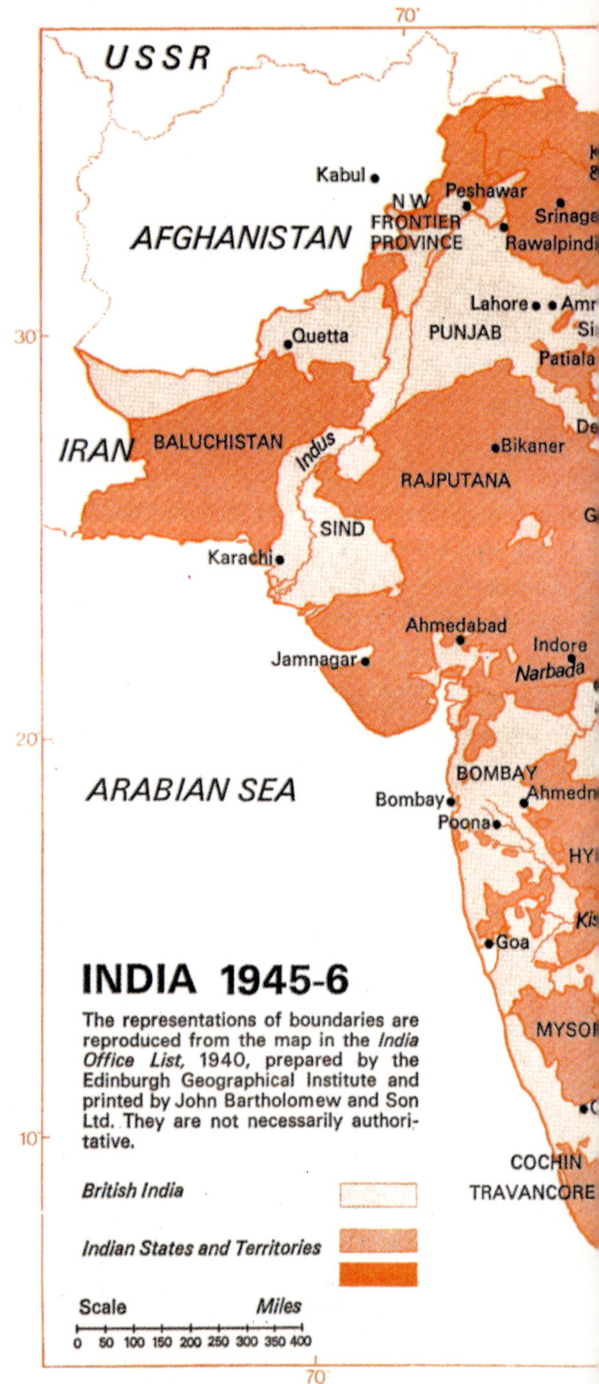

With acknowledgement to "The Transfer of Power 1942-7", Vol.VI. E

India

ief Nicholas Mansergh, Her Majesty's Stationery Office, London, 1976

Junagadh and Kathiawar

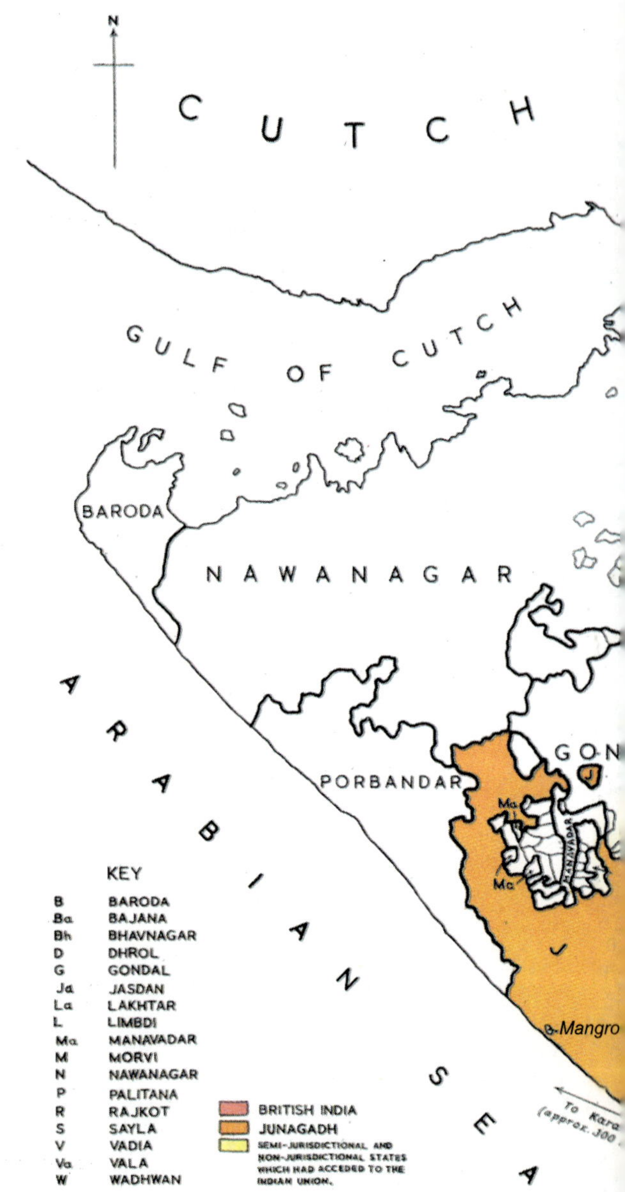

With acknowledgement to "The Story of the Integr

e Western India States Agency

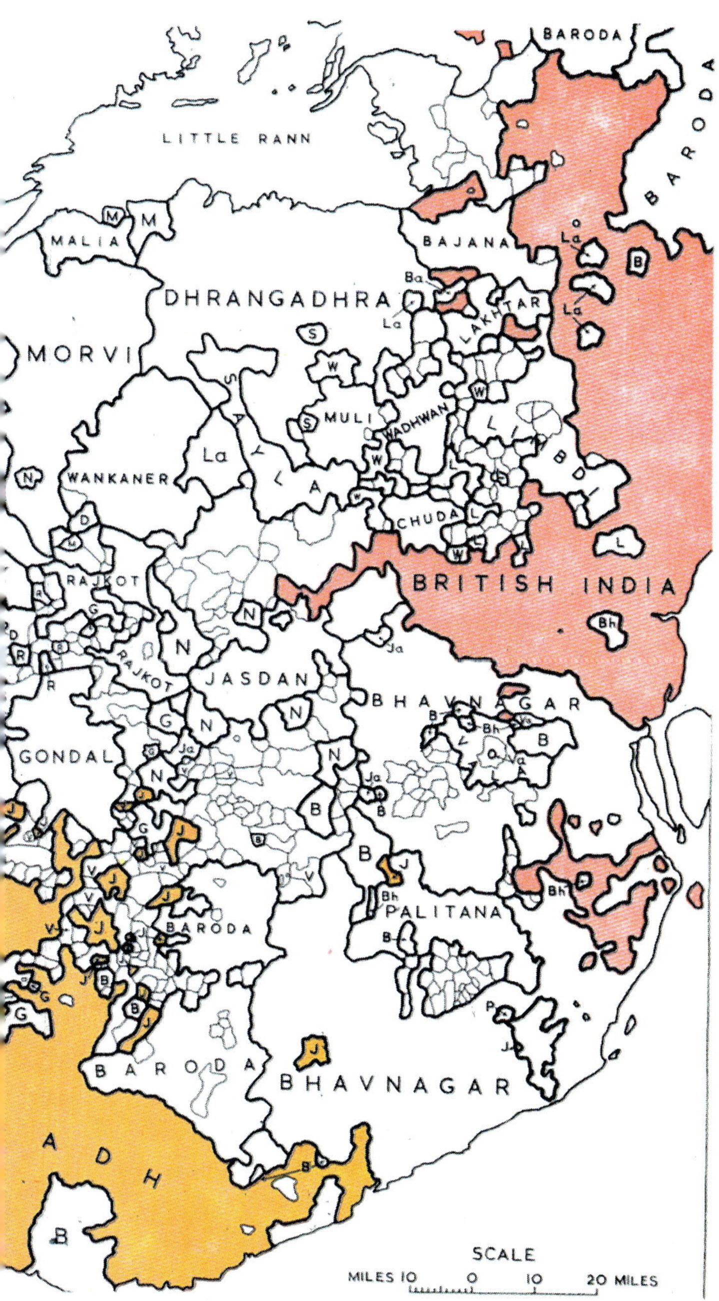

Indian States" by V.P. Menon (Orient Longman, Delhi,1956).

(Depicting th

(Chitral)

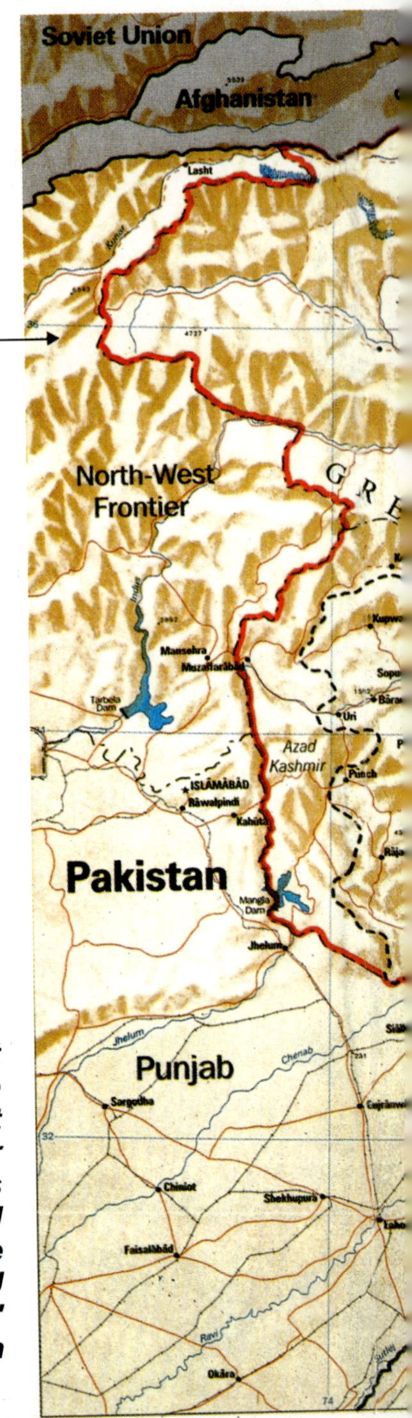

This American map, without any credit line, was distributed at a US Institute for Peace Conference on J&K held just outside Washington D.C. in October 1991. It incorrectly depicts the LOC as running northeast from what is NJ 9842 to a point just west of the Karakoram Pass. A line drawn from NJ 9842 "thence north to the glaciers" would locate most of the Siachen glacier on the Indian side of the LOC.

Kashmir Region

Fire Line/Line of Control, Siachen and Shaksgam)